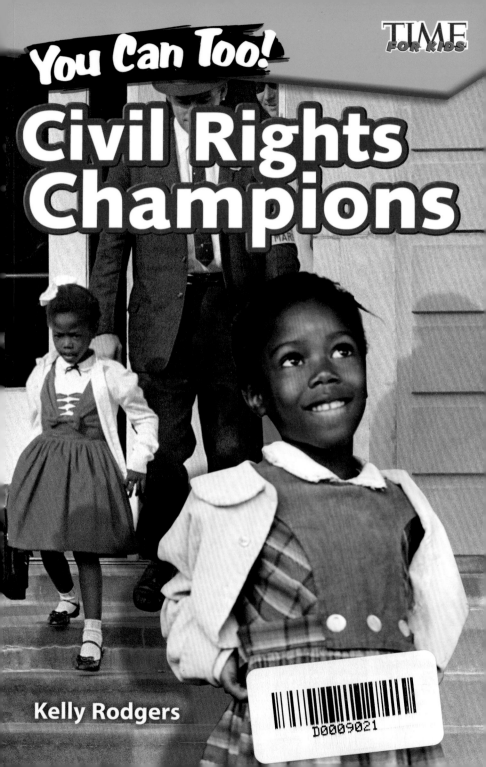

You Can Too!

Civil Rights Champions

TIME FOR KIDS

Kelly Rodgers

D0009021

Table of Contents

Fair and Just

Do you think about *fairness*? Do you know what *justice* means? These two words are very important.

Fairness means treating people with respect. It means making sure everyone has the same chance. It means no one is treated badly.

Justice is about being fair. It means everyone is treated in the same way. People use rules and laws to be just.

Fairness and justice matter. They give everyone the same chance to succeed. But gaining **civil rights** is hard work.

Martin Luther King Jr. fought for civil rights.

Be a Civil Rights Champ!

You can make a difference. Treat all people the same. Make sure to include everyone. Respect others' ideas. And always play by the rules.

The First Americans

American Indians were the first to live in what we now call America. Then, new settlers came to North America. They wanted land and made their own laws. They were not fair to the native people.

The lives of American Indians changed forever. The government did not respect their rights. They had to leave their homes. Their land no longer belonged to them. Then, they lost their right to make important choices about their lives. They were not able to decide where they would live. But they stood up for themselves. They spoke out about their problems.

The Longest Walk

In 1978, many American Indians walked across the United States. They started in San Francisco, California. They ended in Washington, DC. It took them five months. They wanted to remind everyone of all they had lost.

They did not back down. They marched and **protested**. Finally, in 1968, a new law was passed. It was the Indian Civil Rights Act.

It promised American Indians rights. The new law gave them freedom of speech. It gave them freedom to worship. It gave them protection. The law was a beginning, but it was not enough.

American Indians still fight for the right to make their own choices. Their voices deserve to be heard.

A True Warrior

Clyde Warrior was an Oklahoma Ponca Indian. He founded the National Indian Youth Council. He fought for American Indian **traditions**. In 1968, he gave an important speech. It was called "We Are Not Free."

The crowd listens and rests at the end of The Longest Walk, in 1978.

Justice for All

The United States is a nation of laws. Each person is supposed to be equal under the law. That is what justice means. The color of our skin should not matter. But this is not always the case.

Many people have faced **racism**. This is the idea that one group of people is better than another. African Americans face racism. Others do too. In the past, some states had laws separating people by the color of their skin. Only certain people could vote.

An Important Case

The U.S. Supreme Court is the top court in the country. In 1954, the court ruled that segregation in public schools was against the law. Black children and white children would now be able to go to school together.

Rosa Parks Takes a Seat

One day in 1955, Rosa Parks got on a bus to go home after work. Soon, the bus filled up. A white man asked her to give him her seat. She said no and was arrested. Her act of bravery forever changed the country.

African Americans could not shop in the same stores as white Americans. They could not go to the same schools. They could not worship in the same churches. They could not even drink from the same water fountains.

This made many people angry. They decided to do something about it. They started a **movement**. It was called the *civil rights movement*. People joined in to fight for justice. They used words and actions as their weapons. They made speeches. They marched through the streets.

A young boy drinks from a "colored" fountain.

Jackie Robinson at Bat

Today, baseball teams have players of all races. But in the past, African American and white athletes did not play on the same teams. Jackie Robinson changed that. He joined the Dodgers in 1947. He led the way for others.

The Story of Ruby Bridges

In 1960, Ruby Bridges was six years old. The law said Ruby could go to any school she wanted. But that was not happening in Louisiana. Ruby had to take a test. She had to prove she knew enough to go to the same school as white children. Ruby passed the test.

People were angry about this. Her parents were worried. They were afraid for Ruby. But she was brave. She went to school anyway. Four police officers protected her when she went to school. She was the first African American to **integrate** a primary school in the South.

Honored by a President

In 2001, President Bill Clinton honored Ruby Bridges. He invited her to the White House. He honored her for fighting for civil rights. He gave her a medal.

A Brilliant IDEA

Some people cannot see or hear. Some people cannot walk. Sometimes people are born this way, and other times something happens to cause it. People can have **disabilities**.

People with disabilities want to go to school. They want to be able to go places where everyone else goes. They want to do what everyone else does. But, for a long time, they could not. They did not have the same rights.

Disability Rights Champ

Ed Roberts attended high school in the 1950s mostly over the telephone. He could not get his wheelchair into the school building. He fought to get a diploma. He started groups for disability rights at his college in California.

Bethany Hamilton: Survivor

Bethany Hamilton is a surfer in Hawaii. When she was 13, she was attacked by a shark. She lost her left arm. She was back on her surfboard a month later. She inspires athletes everywhere.

In the 1960s, people with disabilities started to fight for their rights. They started a movement. It was similar to the civil rights movement. They worked together. They talked to lawmakers. They wanted to be heard.

In 1975, a new law was passed. It said that all children could go to public school. Schools needed to help all children learn. Children with disabilities were part of this. In 1990, the law became known as IDEA. Other laws passed too. They make sure people with disabilities are treated fairly.

A President with Polio

Franklin D. Roosevelt (at right) had a disease called polio. His body became weak. Then, he could no longer walk. In 1932, Roosevelt was elected U.S. president. His disability did not get in his way.

Breaking Down Barriers

When Lex Frieden was in college, he was in a car accident. He broke his neck. After that, he could not walk. Lex had to use a wheelchair. His doctors told him he could still do the same things everyone else could do. Lex knew this was true, but it would take courage.

Lex went back to college. He broke down **barriers**. He helped other people deal with their disabilities. In Washington, DC, he met with lawmakers. He told them all people deserved to make lives for themselves.

AL ACCESS, EQUAL OPPORT
IVERSARY OF THE AMERICANS WITH DISA

I AM
OLMSTEAD

On His Own

In the 1970s, Lex visited many states. He said that people with disabilities could live on their own. People agreed with him. They asked him to keep fighting. Lex has received awards. He has led many groups. These groups help people with disabilities.

Girl Power

Learning makes life better. It helps you be successful. Every child should be able to get an education. For kids all over the world, going to school makes a big difference.

In many countries today, boys and girls go to the same schools. All children have the same chance to learn. But in some countries, girls are not allowed to go to school. People are trying to change that.

Malala Fund

Malala Yousafzai (mah-LAH-luh yoo-sahf-ZAY) is a hero for education. She fights to make sure all children can go to school. She started the Malala Fund. This group raises money to help boys and girls receive 12 years of schooling.

Girls and boys attend school in Amman, Jordan.

Some kids do not go to school because they have to work. Other kids live too far away from the school. In many countries, going to school costs money. Some parents cannot afford to send their children to school.

Graça Machel (GRAH-suh mah-SHEHL) has worked for equality for girls for many years. She is known around the world for her work. She belongs to a group called "The Elders." This group includes people from all over the world. They fight for the rights of girls and women.

Work to Be Done

Around the world, over 130 million girls are not in school. Women who get a full education are more successful. They are more likely to send their own daughters to school.

Graça Machel speaks at a summit in 2014.

Make a Difference

Everyone should have the same chance to succeed. No one should face unfairness. No one should face **injustice**. But it happens all too often. Remember, each person can make a difference.

How can you help? Speak out against unfairness. When you see injustice, tell someone. Take action. You can be a civil rights champion, too!

A Shining Beacon

People from around the world want to come to America. The United States is a nation of immigrants. President Barack Obama said, "We did not raise the Statue of Liberty with her back to the world. We did it with her light shining as a beacon to the world."

People take the oath to become U.S. citizens.

Glossary

barriers—anything that limits movement or access

civil rights—rights to equality and freedom

disabilities—conditions that keep people from doing certain things

injustice—unfair treatment

integrate—combine into a whole

movement—a series of activities working toward a common goal

protested—fought against something that is wrong or unfair

racism—not accepting others because of their race

traditions—beliefs and customs that are handed down

Index

Check It Out!

Books

Coles, Robert. 2010. The Story of Ruby Bridges. Scholastic Paperbacks.

Maestro, Betsy. 1996. Coming to America: The Story of Immigration. Scholastic Press.

Videos

HBO. *Mighty Times: The Legacy of Rosa Parks*.

Sony Pictures Entertainment. *Soul Surfer*.

Websites

Ducksters. *Civil Rights for Kids*. www.ducksters.com/history/civil _rights/.

Publishing Credits

Rachelle Cracchiolo, M.S.Ed., *Publisher*
Conni Medina, M.A.Ed., *Managing Editor*
Nika Fabienke, Ed.D., *Series Developer*
June Kikuchi, *Content Director*
John Leach, *Assistant Editor*
Lee Aucoin, *Senior Graphic Designer*

TIME For Kids and the TIME For Kids logo are registered trademarks of TIME Inc. Used under license.

Image Credits: Cover and p.1 (front) Bettman/Getty Images, (back) Associated Press; Reader's Guide page Bettmann/Getty Images; p.5 Library of Congress [LC-USZ62-122985]; pp.7, 9 Arthur Grace/ZUMAPRESS/ Newscom; p.11 Granger, NYC; p.12 Library of Congress [LC-DIG-fsa-8a03228]; p.13 National Baseball Hall of Fame Library/MLB Photos via Getty Images; p.15 Associated Press; p.19 Franklin D. Roosevelt Presidential Library & Museum; p.21 AP Photo/Houston Chronicle, Karen Warren; p.23 Ton Koene/VWPics/Alamy Stock Photo; p.25 Lucas Jackson/ Reuters; p.27 Lucas Jackson/Reuters; p.31 Library of Congress [LC-DIG-ds-04000]; all other images from iStock and/or Shutterstock

Library of Congress Cataloging-in-Publication Data

Names: Rodgers, Kelly, author.
Title: You can too! civil rights champions / Kelly Rodgers.
Description: Huntington Beach, CA : Teacher Created Materials, [2018] | Includes index.
Identifiers: LCCN 2017013460 (print) | LCCN 2017029614 (ebook) | ISBN 9781425853440 (eBook) | ISBN 9781425849702 (pbk.)
Subjects: LCSH: Civil rights--Juvenile literature. | Human rights--Juvenile literature.
Classification: LCC JC571 (ebook) | LCC JC571 .R6573 2018 (print) | DDC 323--dc23
LC record available at https://lccn.loc.gov/2017013460

Teacher Created Materials

5301 Oceanus Drive
Huntington Beach, CA 92649-1030
http://www.tcmpub.com

ISBN 978-1-4258-4970-2

© 2018 Teacher Created Materials, Inc.

You Can Too!
Civil Rights Champions

Kelly Rodgers